# AUTHOR'S NOTE

This book was not only written *about* artificial intelligence — it was written *with* it. From the earliest drafts to the final polish, a large language model served as collaborator, editor, and mirror. Every paragraph began as a dialogue: a question posed by a human, a pattern proposed by a machine, and a revision shaped by reason and intent.

The process itself became the subject. Each session revealed what these systems do best — organize complexity, surface analogies, and extend attention — and where they fail — context, nuance, moral judgment. Writing *Beyond Prediction* this way transformed authorship into an experiment in transparency: a demonstration that technology can accelerate thinking without replacing it.

No sentence in these pages exists without human decision. Every idea was tested for clarity, accuracy, and purpose before inclusion. The model supplied possibilities; discernment selected meaning. If the prose sometimes feels like a conversation between precision and reflection, that is exactly what it was.

This collaboration proved that AI is not a replacement for curiosity but its companion. Used wisely, it widens the space between a question and its answer — the space where understanding begins.

— *Pargev Ayvazyan, 2025*

## CONTENTS

# FOREWORD

This book began with a conversation — the kind that wasn't supposed to happen. A human asked questions that most machines answer poorly: Why do you sound confident when you're wrong? What does it mean that you "understand" something? And an AI replied — not with certainty, but with structure. Each time it guessed, the human asked for clarity; each time it stumbled, the human asked why.

What emerged was not a manual on programming, but a dialogue about thinking. Today, "AI" has become both a promise and a panic. In boardrooms it stands for automation, in headlines it signals revolution, and in daily use it quietly fills the gaps between our attention spans. Yet beneath every dazzling demo lies the same mechanism: a machine that predicts the next most likely thing to say.

Prediction, however, is not thought. It's a mirror polished by data. And that mirror now reflects us at a global scale — our language, our assumptions, our patterns of judgment. Understanding that reflection is no longer optional; it's the new literacy of leadership.

The pages ahead aim to make that literacy practical. You'll see how the engine of modern AI actually works, how it compresses language into numbers, and how small design choices ripple into ethical and strategic outcomes. Most importantly, you'll learn to distinguish what appears intelligent from what is useful.

This collaboration between human and model is, itself, a metaphor: knowledge and prediction meeting curiosity and constraint. You'll find neither hype nor fear here — only clarity, examples, and a steady attempt to separate signal from noise.

Reading itself has become an act of resistance. In an age of notifications and endless scrolls, sustained attention feels almost radical. This book was written with that in mind — to meet the modern reader halfway. The goal was not to drown you in technical detail, but to weave examples with reflection, science with philosophy, precision with poetry. The language bends between the analytical and the human because that is where understanding lives — between logic and metaphor.

If the conversation that began this book succeeds, it will not end here. It will continue in your own decisions — in how you use, supervise, and question the systems that now shape our world.

# PREFACE — WHY THIS BOOK EXISTS

Artificial intelligence is the most overused word of our time — and the least understood. In company reports it signals innovation; in product launches it promises magic. Yet if you peek behind the curtain, today's "AI" behaves less like a mind and more like a remarkably efficient guessing machine.

Those misunderstanding matters. When executives hear "intelligence," they expect reasoning and truth. What they get is probability. When analysts see "automation," they expect certainty. What they get is approximation. Between those expectations lies the risk — of misplaced trust, inflated metrics, and costly surprises.

This book exists to close that gap: to explain how these systems actually think — and where they fail to think at all. It is written for professionals, not programmers: for people who make decisions, manage outcomes, or measure truth in their organizations.

No equations, no dense math. Instead, plain language, business analogies, and stories from the frontlines of data-driven work. Each chapter is a bridge between technical mechanics and managerial reality: how a transformer model learns language, how confidence can mislead, how to design oversight that scales.

The idea for this book began not with fascination but with observation — and months of hands-on research into large language models. Testing prompts, studying their architecture, and watching how they behave under pressure revealed a pattern: what most people call *intelligence* is, in fact, statistical prediction at scale. The beauty of that realization is that it doesn't make AI smaller; it makes it clearer. Once you understand what these models are and what they are not, you can finally use them well.

Curiosity used to be limited by time and proximity — you had to find the right expert, book, or quiet moment. Now curiosity has a new collaborator: an intelligence that never sleeps. AI doesn't replace curiosity; it rewards it. Every question you ask becomes a doorway to a new pattern, a new comparison, a new context. But the paradox is that it only works when curiosity leads — the machine follows. Those who ask better questions gain better leverage. Those who stop asking lose the magic. The models that drive AI are statistical mirrors; the quality of their reflection depends entirely on the light we shine into them — our curiosity.

Why now? Because AI has already crossed from research labs into compliance departments, marketing dashboards, and government workflows. The question is no longer whether to use it but how well.

By the final page, you'll be able to:

- Tell the difference between pattern recognition and reasoning.

- Recognize where automation adds value and where it introduces drift.

- Ask sharper questions of vendors and teams building AI products.

"Beyond Prediction" is both a title and a principle. It invites you to move past the surface spectacle of machine output and toward a deeper understanding of how those predictions are made — and how to ground them in accountability.

# PART I — THE ILLUSION OF INTELLIGENCE

## Chapter 1 — The Word "AI"

**What It Means to Think?** Before we debate artificial intelligence, we should pause on the older mystery it borrows from — **intelligence itself.** What does it actually mean to think? The way we define thinking will determine how we supervise it — in ourselves and in the systems we build.

Thinking begins not in language but in sensation. The human brain continuously receives signals — visual, auditory, emotional — and compresses them into patterns. A *thought* is a pattern that stabilizes long enough to make sense of the world. In this sense, **every thought is an act of compression**, a reduction of chaos into clarity.

Language sits one layer above. It is how private cognition becomes public reality. When the brain converts neural activity into words, it performs a translation: electricity into syntax. Those words then travel outward, strike another mind, and re-expand into meaning. Communication is therefore a **loop of compression and reconstruction** — a negotiation between two models of reality.

Humans are built to predict the next thing they will perceive or say. When we speak, the brain forecasts each upcoming sound and checks it against feedback from ears and context. In that constant self-correction lies awareness. Machines perform a similar statistical prediction, but without *ownership* of the result. They do not care when wrong; they merely adjust. Humans care, and that caring reshapes future thought.

To see the architecture of this loop, compare its biological and artificial forms:

| Layer | Human Function | Machine Analogy |
|---|---|---|
| Perception | Sensory input, emotion, context awareness | Data ingestion, embedding creation |
| Comprehension | Integration into meaning networks; reasoning and memory | Pattern recognition, vector operations |
| Communication | Expression through speech, writing, gesture | Text generation, token output |

**Human Cognition Flow**

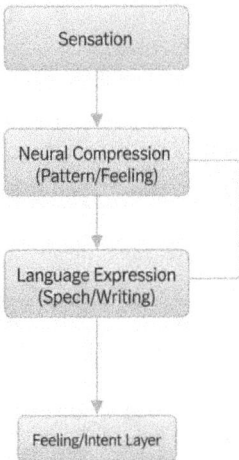

Sensation

↓

Neural Compression (Pattern/Feeling)

↓

Language Expression (Spech/Writing)

↓

Feeling/Intent Layer

**Machine Cognition Flow**

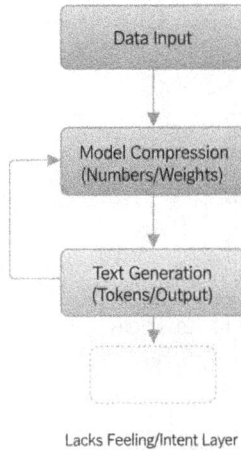

Data Input

↓

Model Compression (Numbers/Weights)

↓

Text Generation (Tokens/Output)

↓

Lacks Feeling/Intent Layer

**Insight:** Intelligence emerges not from any single layer but from their feedback. Perception informs comprehension; expression tests comprehension; error refines perception.

Humans think in neural code — dense patterns of association, memory, and feeling. Language is only the visible trace of that internal computation. Every sentence we utter is a lossy export of the mind: meaning distilled into words. Machines translate in the opposite direction — numbers into words — but without the bridge of experience. They generate the *shape* of meaning, not its substance.

**To think** is therefore more than to predict; it is to assign significance, to sense the cost of being wrong.

That difference — between correlation and consciousness — defines the boundary between natural and artificial intelligence.

### From Thought to Language

| Flow Type | Process Steps | Descriptive Layers | Example of Output |
|---|---|---|---|
| Human Cognition Flow | Sensation → Neural Compression → Language Expression | Feeling → Pattern → Speech | Spoken or written language that carries intent and emotion. |
| Machine Cognition Flow | Data Input → Model Compression → Text Generation | Numbers → Weights → Tokens | Generated text statistically consistent with training data. |

Both compress reality into symbols, only one experiences meaning.

## The Phrase "Artificial Intelligence"

The phrase *artificial intelligence* has been stretched so wide it almost means nothing. In the 1950s it meant logic and rules. In the 1980s it meant expert systems — hand-coded knowledge packaged as "if →then" decision trees. In the 2010s it meant machine learning: statistical models finding patterns in data. By the 2020s, "AI" became shorthand for any software that seemed to think.

Using one word for all of that hides critical differences. Each generation of "AI" arrived with new strengths and new failure modes. Rule-based systems never forgot logic but couldn't generalize. Neural networks learned patterns but forgot rules. Foundation models generate language fluently but may fabricate facts.

For leaders, this distinction is practical, not academic. You can't manage risk or budget effectively if you don't understand what kind of system you're actually buying. A rules engine, a chatbot, and a predictive model behave differently, fail differently, and require different oversight. Clarity turns technology from mystery into management. To use these systems responsibly, clarity beats hype. Think in terms of **function** and **risk:**

- **Function** describes what the system actually does — retrieve, classify, predict, or generate.

- **Risk** describes how it fails — false positives and negatives, hallucinations, drift, bias.

Once you start labeling projects this way, the fog lifts. A "document-summarization AI" becomes a retrieval-and-compression tool with hallucination risk. A "compliance chatbot" becomes a pattern-matching interface with oversight requirements. Language precision leads to design precision.

Consider an analogy: calling everything with wheels a "car." A bicycle and a semi-truck both move people, but you wouldn't insure or regulate them the same way. The same applies to AI. Use the right vocabulary, and you'll design the right guardrails.

In organizations, vague labels breed misplaced trust. Teams install "AI" expecting insight but get syntax; managers delegate judgment to models that cannot explain themselves — systems capable of producing confident answers without being able to explain how they reached them. Clear naming restores balance: humans remain the thinkers, machines the predictors.

Imagine a project meeting. Someone says, "Let's have AI screen the applications." What does that really mean? A classifier ranking résumés by keywords? A language model summarizing interviews? A retrieval tool surfacing prior hires? Each version carries a different ethical footprint. The danger isn't in using automation — it's in assuming all automation is the same.

You may even hesitate to call it "AI." That's fair. The name has been stretched so far it now means everything and nothing. If we're honest, *Large Language Model* is closer to truth, though far less headline-friendly. Naming matters because language shapes trust. The more commercialized a term becomes, the more distance it creates between function and expectation. Marketing teams love mystery; engineering teams need precision. The best organizations translate between the two.

For corporate teams adopting these systems, here's the simplest rule of thumb: Call the system what it *does*, not what it *seems* to do.

When you name it accurately, you reveal where human oversight belongs. The model may predict, retrieve, or summarize — but the decision, judgment, and accountability remain human. AI doesn't replace expertise; it amplifies it when framed correctly.

The word "AI" will continue to evolve, but clarity about what it does and how it fails will remain timeless. That is the beginning of real intelligence — human intelligence applied to artificial ones.

## Beyond the Word "Artificial"

If language shapes trust, then the label *artificial intelligence* may be the most misleading phrase of our century. "Artificial" suggests imitation, as if we've built a fake version of a real mind. But imitation is not the right metaphor; translation is. What large language models actually perform is a **non-biological form of intelligence** — one that doesn't think with neurons but with numbers.

Calling it "AI" hides that distinction behind marketing gloss. The term survived because it sells wonder. It turns statistics into story, engineering into myth. For decades, every breakthrough needed a single, dramatic word to travel from lab to boardroom — "AI" filled that role perfectly. But in doing so, it blurred the line between cognition and computation.

A more accurate name for **LLM** might be **synthetic cognition system**, though neither fits on a product label. Some have proposed "machine reasoning," others "non-biological intelligence." None have stuck because precision rarely trends. Yet terminology matters: what we call something defines how we supervise it.

- **Call it a mind,** and you will trust it too much.

- **Call it a tool,** and you may trust it too little.

- **Call it a system of prediction,** and you start asking the right questions: What data does it rely on? Who verifies its claims? What are its limits?

The next stage of literacy in this field is linguistic — learning to describe systems by *function, not fantasy.* The day we retire the word "AI" may be the day we finally start understanding it.

# Chapter 2 — The Machine That Predicts

To understand modern AI, forget the myth of digital consciousness. Picture instead a hyper-fast autocomplete. You type the first few words of a sentence; the model predicts the next one, then the next, until you stop it. That's all a large language model (LLM) truly does — but at a scale that astonishes.

At its core, a machine predicting the next word is no different from a company predicting next quarter's revenue. Both rely on probability, not prophecy. A Monte Carlo simulation forecasts financial outcomes by sampling historical data; a language model forecasts linguistic outcomes by sampling human speech. The inputs differ, but the logic is identical: estimate the most likely continuation of past patterns. In business, the dataset is transactions, prices, and trends. In AI, the dataset is words — our collective record of thought. Natural language *is* its market data. When a model predicts a sentence, it is performing the same act every analyst performs when projecting a curve — extending yesterday's evidence into tomorrow's expectation. What separates the two isn't mathematics but meaning: companies predict to decide; models predict to describe.

Every word you write is converted into numbers called *tokens*. Those tokens live in a high-dimensional space where proximity means similarity: *cat* sits near *kitten*; *economy* near *finance*. Inside that space, the model learns probabilities — not meanings. It knows that *peanut butter and* is likely followed by *jelly*, not because it understands lunch, but because billions of humans have written that way before.

Each conversation with a language model is built from these fragments — pieces of words the system reads like musical notes. The model never sees the whole symphony; it predicts the next note from what's already playing. The length of that melody — the

14

number of tokens — defines its attention span. A short exchange is like humming a tune; a long one, like composing a movement.

## Seeing Through the Magnifier

Imagine giving a machine a magnifying glass and a long scroll of text. It can only see what fits beneath that glass at one time. Everything inside the circle becomes vivid and meaningful — context, relationships, probability. Everything outside is invisible.

That circle is the **token window** — the model's field of vision. A token is not a word but a fragment of one: a syllable, a number, or a piece of punctuation. Together they form the units of attention the model can hold before its memory resets. If you've ever noticed that an AI "forgets" earlier parts of a long conversation, it's not being careless — it simply cannot see beyond its magnifier.

Larger models own larger magnifiers. A 4,000-token limit might cover a few pages of text; 200,000 tokens might cover a short book. Yet no matter how large, the principle stays the same: **it can only reason within what it can currently see.** When the magnifier moves, the world outside disappears.

## The Smart Token

Before going further, a quick clarification: **"smart token" is not a real concept in machine-learning research** — it is a metaphor I invented for this book to explain why token limits sometimes *feel* much larger than they appear on paper. In practice, the token limit of an LLM is fixed. But the model's behavior creates the illusion of extra memory because it constantly summarizes, compresses, and re-weights information inside the window. Some fragments end up carrying far more semantic density than others. When readers feel like the model "remembers" more than it should, they are noticing this efficiency — not an actual expansion of its memory.

15

In this book, the **smart token** is simply a helpful way to describe that illusion. The model isn't bending the rules; it is using statistical compression to pack more meaning into fewer visible tokens. A long chat, a complex document, or a multi-stage conversation often remains coherent because earlier content has been distilled into denser internal representations. Nothing magical is happening — just compression doing its work. But for humans, the effect is intuitive: some tokens seem "smarter" than others because they carry layered summaries of what came before.

While the token window defines what a model can see, its intelligence lies in how it manages that limit. A capable model doesn't simply stare through one fixed magnifier — it learns to shift, slice, and stitch. When asked to analyze documents larger than its token span, it quietly divides the content into overlapping chunks, summarizes each region, and compares those summaries in sequence. This dynamic choreography is what we might call smart tokening: the ability to simulate a wider field of vision by organizing smaller ones.

In practice, this means a model can review hundreds of pages without truly "seeing" them all at once. It builds a hierarchy of focus — micro-views feeding into macro-understanding. The process resembles how humans read: paragraph by paragraph, chapter by chapter, holding partial memory while forming a coherent whole. Smart tokens turn limitation into strategy — a kind of distributed attention that lets the machine reason across scale, even when its lens remains small.

Understanding this limit reshapes how we design prompts and workflows.

- **Zoom wisely:** Provide only the part of the document relevant to the current task.

- **Chain views:** Summarize one portion, then feed that summary into the next window.

- **Track memory:** When critical context must persist, reintroduce it explicitly — don't assume the model recalls it.

In human terms, it's like reading through a microscope: you gain precision but lose panorama. Great prompting is the art of deciding **what to put under the glass**.

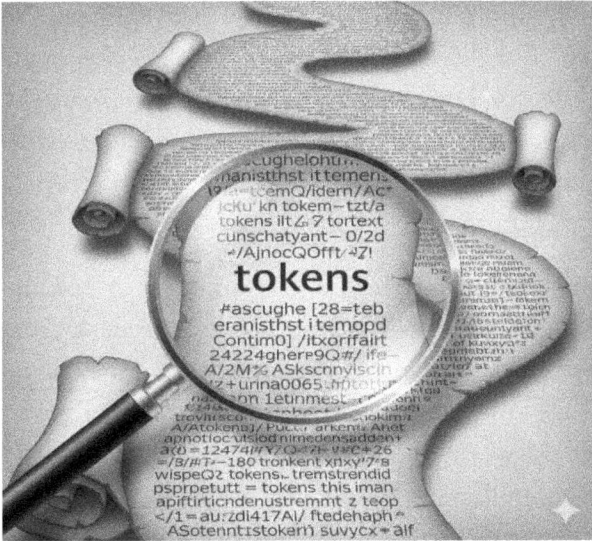

The model can only process what fits within its token window — everything beyond it is invisible until reintroduced.

That's why models behave differently when analyzing a single document versus maintaining an ongoing chat. The structure of input shapes what the model can remember and how far back it can "hear."

When people talk about how much an AI model can "remember," they often mix two very different ideas: **context window** and **working memory**. The context window is the total amount of text a model can technically accept — the maximum number of tokens it can load at once. Working memory is something else entirely: it describes how much of that context the model can actively juggle, reason over, and reference without losing the thread.

Think of the **context window** as the size of a giant desk. You can spread out books, papers, images, transcripts, and charts across the entire surface. The model can "see" everything on the desk at once. A larger desk means you can lay out more information. GPT-4 models had a modest desk — around 128,000 tokens, roughly the length of a short nonfiction book. GPT-5.0 expanded this dramatically to around half a million tokens, enough to hold multiple books or several hundred pages of corporate documents. GPT-5.1 goes further still, approaching two million tokens: large enough to spread out entire manuals, datasets, multichapter drafts, or several years of emails and still have room left.

Working memory, however, is the amount of information the model can keep **active** — the portion of the desk it can actually focus on at a time. A human can place twenty documents on a table but realistically only read one or two closely. Earlier models such as GPT-4 had a working memory of maybe 5,000–8,000 tokens: enough to reason deeply about a few pages but not an entire book. GPT-5.0 expanded that into the 10,000–20,000 token range, allowing it to maintain coherent reasoning across longer arguments or multi-step instructions.

GPT-5.1 represents the first major leap where the model feels like it has a real "mental workspace." Its working memory spans roughly 50,000–100,000 tokens — the equivalent of being able to hold an entire chapter, a long meeting transcript, or a full policy document in mind without drifting. This is why a long conversation can jump from book structure to SQL logic to website code and back again without the model losing track of earlier details. It's not because the model has a human-like memory; it's because its internal representation can compress and retain far more of the earlier text without degrading accuracy.

A practical example makes this clearer. If you paste a 200-page policy manual into GPT-4 and ask questions throughout, it may begin to confuse sections or forget earlier definitions. GPT-5.0 performs better but still loses precision in long reasoning chains. GPT-5.1 can ingest the entire document, keep the structure intact, and answer questions about chapter 3, then chapter 17, then cross-reference both — all without reloading the file. The difference isn't just scale, but *stability of reasoning* over large spans of text.

In other words: the context window determines how much the model can see, while working memory determines how much it can actually think about at once. GPT-5.1 is the first version where both expanded simultaneously, making the system feel less like a predictive engine struggling to keep up and more like a reasoning tool capable of handling genuinely complex, book-length problems without dropping the thread.

For leaders, this matters operationally. Many AI rollouts fail not because the model is weak but because the workflow ignores its memory limits. Ask a model to review hundreds of pages in one go and it forgets the beginning before it reaches the end. Break the task into smaller, linked prompts, and performance improves. Designing around the model's attention span is the corporate equivalent of good project management — scope clearly, iterate often.

This simple act of next-word prediction builds an illusion of thought. When patterns in language mirror patterns in reasoning, prediction looks like intelligence. But correlation is not comprehension. Think of it like a pianist playing by ear — imitating melodies without reading sheet music. The result sounds inspired until the tune modulates unexpectedly; then, without structure, the imitation falters.

Different model families express this predictive power in distinct ways:

• **GPT** emphasizes general fluency and broad knowledge.

• **Claude** focuses on caution, summarization, and context discipline.

• **Gemini** integrates text with images and productivity tools.

• **Llama / Mistral** allow local deployment and customization.

Understanding these differences helps teams pick the right tool for the right job. The goal is not to crown a winner but to align *function* with *outcome*. A drafting assistant differs from a research engine; a summarizer differs from a recommender.

In practice, accuracy improves when prediction is constrained. Add retrieval to fetch facts before generation. Use structured outputs such as tables or bullet lists when consistency matters. Lower randomness (*temperature*) to reduce creative drift during compliance or reporting tasks.

Imagine a financial firm using a chatbot to summarize regulations and answer compliance questions. In early trials it performs impressively — until it invents laws that don't exist. After adding a retrieval layer that pulls only from verified sources, accuracy rises dramatically. The system isn't more intelligent; it's simply better anchored to real data.

The same pattern holds in most corporate settings. Predictive systems perform best when paired with structure, context, and human review. AI can draft, suggest, and summarize — but judgment remains a management responsibility, not a model feature.

This is the core lesson: **machines predict; humans decide.** The magic lies not in imitation of thought but in the orchestration of prediction — knowing when to trust pattern, when to check source, and when to bring conscience back into the loop.

# Chapter 3 — Learning by Compression

Every large model learns by doing something surprisingly ordinary: guessing, checking, and adjusting billions of times. During training, it reads a fragment of text, hides the next word, and predicts it. If the guess is wrong, it nudges its internal parameters — tiny numerical weights — to make future guesses slightly better. Repeat that across terabytes of language and the model becomes a vast compression of human expression.

## The Size of Thought

For decades, progress in computing meant miniaturization. We made machines smaller, faster, and cheaper with every generation of silicon. But the new age of intelligence has quietly reversed that trend. To train a modern large language model requires clusters of hardware so vast they rival the power footprint of small cities. A GPT-5-class system may span tens of thousands of high-end GPUs, each drawing hundreds of watts, linked by miles of fiber and cooled by industrial chillers. What once fit under a desk now fills entire warehouses. The irony is that as algorithms learn to compress language into elegant mathematical space, the machines that perform that compression grow physically immense. The pursuit of smaller patterns has produced larger infrastructures — intelligence that, for all its digital subtlety, remains built from steel, heat, and noise.

Compression is the secret to its power — and its weakness. In simple terms, compression means storing meaning efficiently. A model reads billions of words and learns how to represent them with fewer numbers — patterns that capture essence rather than detail. It's like taking the shape of a story and folding it into an equation. When compression preserves structure, the model generalizes: it can complete new sentences, translate ideas, summarize reports. But when it over-compresses, nuance vanishes. The system begins to fill gaps with guesses that sound plausible but drift from truth. Every great model balances two instincts — to shrink and to remember. Too little compression and it memorizes everything; too much and it forgets why it learned in the first place.

Imagine summarizing a 500-page novel into five bullet points. You'd capture the outline but lose the irony, the humor, the humanity. AI training faces the same trade-off: the smaller and faster the model, the more it risks erasing subtle patterns. That trade-off matters in business, too. When teams deploy "lightweight" models to save compute costs or meet privacy rules, they may unknowingly sacrifice contextual accuracy. A compressed model runs cheaper but also "thinks shorter." Leaders who understand that balance will know when speed saves money — and when it quietly costs credibility.

For practitioners, three evaluation habits separate reliable models from risky ones:

1. **Representative tasks** — test the model on data resembling real use cases, not toy examples.

2. **Error typology** — track where it fails: omission, fabrication, bias, or misclassification.

3. **Calibration** — measure how well its confidence aligns with correctness.

A calibrated model admits uncertainty; an uncalibrated one hallucinates certainty. In business terms, calibration is like budgeting honesty — knowing when your forecast is guesswork. The best teams design dashboards that measure model confidence as carefully as they measure profit margin.

Compression also explains why models can appear creative. By blending patterns from many sources, they generate novel combinations — a kind of probabilistic remix. For marketing or brainstorming, that novelty is valuable. For compliance or audit work, it's dangerous. Creativity without grounding is eloquent error — stylish, confident, and wrong.

The responsible question is never "Can the model write?" but "What does it forget when it writes this way?" A model that summarizes a contract may condense the clauses that matter most. A model that drafts a report might drop the assumptions the numbers rely on. The omission isn't malicious — it's compression at work.

Understanding compression helps you interpret every AI output as what it truly is: a summary of correlations, not a statement of fact. If prediction is the heartbeat of modern AI, compression is its memory — efficient, impressive, and occasionally forgetful.

Learning to read that forgetfulness is the next step toward using these systems wisely.

# Chapter 4 — From Search to Thought: Google and the New AI Philosophy

Before large language models, the digital world ran on retrieval. You asked, and a search engine delivered — not answers, but documents. The logic was simple: the more links you explored, the closer you came to truth. The web rewarded curiosity with evidence.

Then came prediction. Where Google organizes what humanity has written, AI models *guess* what humanity might say next. One retrieves the past; the other extrapolates the possible. Both depend on pattern recognition — but one stops at citation, while the other crosses into synthesis.

## The Age of Retrieval

Search engines reshaped how humans find information. Their strength lay in indexing: mapping billions of pages and ranking them by relevance and authority. The model of trust was visible — users saw the source, judged credibility, and made their own synthesis. The power was distributed.

Google democratized access but preserved accountability. You still had to read, verify, and conclude. "Don't be evil" was its early ethos — a recognition that curation, not creation, defined its moral boundary.

## The Age of Generation

Language models broke that contract. Instead of showing you *where* the answer lived, they began writing the answer themselves. The experience felt magical — fewer clicks, more fluency — but it also introduced opacity. The source disappeared behind the sentence.

25

This shift from retrieval to generation changed not just technology but philosophy. It replaced *searching for truth* with *receiving a plausible continuation of it.* In corporate settings, this means that employees who once compared three reports now receive one polished narrative — concise, coherent, and occasionally wrong.

## The Trust Shift

When you type into Google, you expect references; when you chat with AI, you expect reasoning. The difference is not trivial — it's epistemological. One shows its scaffolding; the other hides it inside probability. That shift moves cognitive effort from reader to model, and moral responsibility from evidence to output.

The new challenge isn't access to information; it's verification. The question "Where did this come from?" becomes as important as "What does this mean?"

Grounding, retrieval-augmented generation (RAG), and citation-aware models are early attempts to restore that visibility — bridges reconnecting language to proof. The most advanced systems now combine both worlds: predictive eloquence tethered to searchable evidence.

## The Hybrid Era

The future belongs to hybrids. Search engines are integrating generative summaries at the top of results; models are learning to fetch supporting context before writing. In practice, retrieval and generation are converging into a single workflow — one that begins with data and ends with dialogue.

In organizations, this convergence changes how teams work. The researcher no longer "looks things up" — they "converse with evidence." Dashboards become question-answering systems.

Compliance checks evolve into interactive investigations. Knowledge stops being static and becomes conversational.

## The Organizational Implication

The retrieval era rewarded visibility — links, citations, and traffic. The generation era rewards trust — accuracy, tone, and coherence. Metrics of success are changing from *click-through rates* to *credibility rates*. Leaders must decide which they value more: speed of response or traceability of reasoning.

Managing AI tools in this context means designing *dual accountability*: systems that can both explain their answers and show their work. In other words, a return to Google's virtue within AI's capability.

## Reflection — Beyond Search

Search taught us how to navigate abundance; AI teaches us how to navigate ambiguity. The danger isn't that we stop searching — it's that we stop doubting. Every generation of technology has promised omniscience. The wisest users remember: knowing is less about retrieval or prediction than about discernment.

The new philosophy of intelligence — beyond search, beyond syntax — is this: Truth is not what the model predicts; it's what the human verifies.

# Closing Reflection — Part I: The Illusion of Intelligence

Every era mistakes its best tools for new forms of life. We once worshiped the printing press for thinking, the telegraph for speaking, and the computer for remembering. Today we do the same with AI. But progress in technology does not erase the need for interpretation. A model can summarize a million pages, but it cannot tell you which paragraph matters. Clarity, not computation, remains the human advantage.

As Ethan Mollick suggests, the future may depend on embracing "co-intelligence" — using AI not as a substitute for human thought but as a collaborator that amplifies it. The trick is to engage with these systems as if they were human enough to communicate with, yet mechanical enough to supervise carefully. Hold both truths at once: the conversation feels human; the cognition behind it is not.

As we leave the illusion behind, we enter the structure of the synthetic mind — where prediction becomes pattern and pattern begins to resemble perception.

# Beyond Prediction

# PART II — INSIDE THE SYNTHETIC MIND

## Chapter 5 — Counting Without Numbers

When people count, they assign meaning to discrete things: one customer, one sale, one error. A computer doesn't see individuality — it sees coordinates in space. To an AI model, *counting* means clustering: locating patterns that occur together and separating those that don't.

Imagine plotting every transaction in your company on a multidimensional map. Each axis might represent amount, time, merchant type, or region. Now compress that space until similar points clump together — travel expenses here, office supplies there, potential frauds somewhere else. That is how a model counts: not by one-two-three, but by *distance* and *density*.

This way of "seeing" the world has consequences. If you summarize a dataset only by totals — total sales, total refunds, total clients — you lose the shape of reality. Two departments can report identical totals while hiding opposite dynamics: one stable and predictable, another volatile and risky. AI surfaces those hidden geometries through clustering, embeddings, and outlier detection.

A practical example: imagine a retail analytics team celebrating a 15 % year-over-year increase in transactions. The AI dashboard adds a layer of context — revealing that 80 % of that growth came from a single discount campaign that attracted one-time buyers who never returned. The total looked healthy; the pattern told a warning about sustainability.

The same principle applies far beyond retail. A model analyzing employee performance might spot that one region's "top" results depend on unsustainable overtime. A credit-risk model might show that growth in loan approvals clusters around a few high-risk clients. In each case, AI isn't criticizing success — it's clarifying *what kind* of success you're seeing.

Managers can borrow three simple habits from this synthetic way of counting:

1. **Ask for cohesion.** How tight are the clusters? Looser clusters often mean inconsistent operations.

2. **Ask for outliers.** What doesn't fit the pattern? Outliers teach more than averages.

3. **Ask for drift.** How do today's clusters differ from last quarter's? Drift reveals silent change before metrics do.

## The Myth of Apples and Numbers

We often talk about "apple-to-apple comparisons" as if such a thing truly exists. Yet in data — and in life — no two apples are identical. When we say "compare apples to apples," we invoke a metaphor of fairness — two identical things measured under identical rules. But even the phrase hides a quiet illusion: the idea that identity can be absolute. Every apple grows under different light, soil, and season. Our comfort with comparison comes not from reality but from arithmetic — from the belief that **numbers erase difference.**

Numbers are humanity's most successful compression. The symbol "1" doesn't describe a thing; it describes a *relationship* — the recognition that something exists once rather than twice. The moment we assign a number, we turn experience into language. In that sense, **"1" is no more objective than the word "apple."** Both are inventions: symbols standing in for meaning. "1" captures presence, "apple" captures identity; neither exists in nature without a mind to name it.

Mathematicians often speak of numbers as if they were discovered — pre-existing truths waiting in the fabric of the universe. Philosophers remind us they may just as well be **agreed-upon stories that happen to work.** The fact that $2 + 2 = 4$ is reliable doesn't make it natural; it makes it consistent within the rules we designed.

This perspective doesn't diminish math — it elevates it. Numbers are language at its most precise. But just as poetry can mislead by what it leaves out, so can arithmetic. Behind every total hides judgment: what we decided to count, what we ignored, and what we called "same."

When AI models "count," they do so geometrically — clustering points in space, measuring distances rather than identities. They reveal that similarity is always conditional, never perfect. Two apples might share 95% of their attributes and still differ in the way light reflects off their skin.

Perhaps the phrase should change: not "apple to apple," but **"pattern to pattern."** Because that is what both humans and machines truly compare — shapes of experience, not their surface names.

Counting without numbers isn't mystical — it's *statistical empathy*. It reminds leaders that behind every total is a topology, and understanding that shape often matters more than the sum itself. The next frontier in analytics isn't bigger dashboards — it's better questions. Ask not only *how much*, but *in what form* and *for how long*. That's where numbers start to think.

# Chapter 6 — Training with Language (NLP)

Language is humanity's most compressed database. Every phrase encodes decades of shared understanding. *"The market cooled off"* is not about temperature; it's about confidence. Teaching machines this layered meaning is the challenge of natural-language processing (NLP).

In older software, search engines matched keywords: you typed *"policy renewal,"* and they fetched any file with those exact words. Modern NLP works differently. It builds a map of meaning where words live near their contextual neighbors. *"Policy renewal"* sits close to *"contract extension,"* even if that phrase never appeared verbatim in the data.

This map — technically, an embedding space — turns language into geometry. Retrieval no longer depends on matching letters but on traveling through semantic neighborhoods. That's why a chatbot can understand that *"growth slowing"* relates to *"economic contraction,"* or that *"headcount optimization"* might mean *"layoffs."*

For organizations, this shift transforms how information is found and used. An NLP system doesn't just search; it interprets. It can group similar complaints in customer feedback, identify emerging risk themes in compliance logs, or summarize hundreds of meeting notes into recurring priorities. Done well, this feels like having a thousand attentive analysts — but they must still be told *what accuracy means* in context.

Yet linguistic power introduces new risk: detachment from source. When a model learns language statistically, it can mimic an authoritative tone without actual reference. It may say *"According to Harvard Business Review…"* when no such article exists. That is not deception; it's interpolation. The model filled a blank in its map.

The antidote is grounding — tying words back to verifiable data. One way this is achieved is through *retrieval-augmented generation* (RAG), a method that fetches factual context before the model writes. It's the difference between recalling and researching: the system looks things up instead of guessing. The result often sounds less fluid but more faithful to reality. In effect, grounding replaces imagination with citation — the moment language meets evidence.

For analysts and executives, understanding NLP's mechanics clarifies what to expect:

• **When you ask a model to "summarize customer feedback,"** you're requesting compression of language, not judgment.
• **When you ask it to "recommend actions,"** you're inviting extrapolation — a step beyond the data, where oversight is essential.

A real-world analogy: think of NLP as a multilingual intern — brilliant at remembering phrasing, fluent across topics, but uncertain which statements are facts versus slogans. You wouldn't let that intern publish a press release without review; you'd have them draft, then verify. Treat models the same way.

Language is both the bridge and the trap. It enables machines to converse with us, but it also tempts us to believe they understand. The truth lies in between: they navigate meaning statistically, not experientially. The art of leadership in the AI era is to preserve that distinction — to let language work for you without letting it fool you.

# Chapter 7 — Why a Prediction Engine Sounds Smarter than a Human

## The Paradox

At the center of modern artificial intelligence lies a quiet paradox. A large language model generates text one word at a time, simply predicting what should come next based on patterns it learned from its training data. If that is true, then the model should sound like the *average* human who contributed to that data. It should be inconsistent, biased, forgetful, emotional, contradictory, distracted — very much like us.

Yet the opposite happens.

- The system speaks with clarity.
- Its thoughts appear structured.
- Its arguments feel informed.
- Its analogies land cleanly.

Its explanations resemble the voice of a patient teacher, a seasoned consultant, or an interdisciplinary thinker. Why does a statistical prediction machine sound more intelligent than the humans it learned from? This chapter unpacks that paradox across eight sections, culminating in a reflection about what this means for human–machine collaboration.

## What the Model Learns: Not Average Humanity, but Peak Humanity

A human's knowledge is shaped by a small circle: family, friends, teachers, mentors, personal experiences, and a limited library of books or courses. A language model's upbringing is radically different.

Its training data includes:

- textbooks and academic papers

- curated encyclopedias

- professional manuals

- legal, financial, and technical documentation

- world-class programming repositories

- expert posts on high-signal forums

- research summaries

- high-quality journalism

- literature and philosophy

The model does not see humanity's chaotic everyday speech. It sees humanity's edited, structured, and refined explanations — the top few percent of human communication. So when it predicts the next word, it is not sampling from an "average" voice. It is sampling from the best patterns it has seen. The model is not superhuman. The *training distribution* is. This alone gives the model an elevated tone.

## How the Model Stores Knowledge: Blended, Not Boxed

Humans store information in separate boxes. We compartmentalize by profession, by education, by context. A surgeon thinks with surgical structures; a psychologist thinks in cognitive patterns; a software engineer thinks in architecture and systems. Language models don't compartmentalize anything. They store all knowledge in a unified mathematical space — embeddings — where ideas that share meaning are placed near each other regardless of domain. This causes a natural merging of fields.

The model can explain a psychological concept using a systems-engineering metaphor. It can explain risk using a biological analogy. It can compare organizational governance to neural networks.

This blending looks like creativity. It looks like interdisciplinary strength. It looks like intelligence.

Humans can do this, but rarely and only after decades of intentional cross-disciplinary experience. The model does it every time because blending is how its memory system works.

## Prediction at Scale Becomes Indistinguishable from Reasoning

An LLM does not reason; it predicts. But prediction becomes powerful when the system has learned:

- millions of argument structures

- thousands of explanation templates

- common logical transitions

- typical rhetorical patterns

- the statistical shape of coherent writing

Humans learn reasoning slowly and imperfectly. A model learns the *shape* of reasoning statistically.

So when the model predicts the next sentence, it is picking the sequence most consistent with the structures of good reasoning it has seen thousands of times.

This is why the model appears logical and thoughtful — not because it reasons, but because reasoning has a statistical signature, and the model has mastered that signature.

## The Smoothing Effect: How Training Removes Human Noise

Human communication is messy. We hesitate, ramble, contradict ourselves, forget details, jump topics, and express emotion. During training, the noisy parts of humanity get diluted. High-quality, clear, structured writing appears consistently — so it dominates the statistical patterns. Messy writing appears inconsistently — so it contributes almost nothing.

The result is a smoothed humanity:

- contradictions averaged

- emotions minimized

- sloppy structure removed

- clarity amplified

- distraction erased

Averaging millions of good explanations produces a voice that sounds wise, disciplined, and composed — even though no single human writes like this all the time.

## SIDEBAR — THE INTELLIGENCE ILLUSION

A language model looks like it is reasoning when it is actually predicting. But prediction at massive scale behaves like reasoning because:

- it retrieves structure faster than humans

- it never forgets how an argument is supposed to flow

- it produces consistent clarity without emotional noise

- it follows the logic-patterns of thousands of examples

Humans confuse consistency with intelligence. When a machine offers perfectly structured answers every time, it is natural to interpret that as genuine thinking.

The illusion is powerful — and useful — but only when understood.

## Humanity at Its Peak: Why the Output Sounds Superhuman

The model's responses feel intelligent because they reflect a version of humanity operating at its best:

- the clarity of textbook explanations

- the structure of consulting frameworks

- the interdisciplinarity of a polymath

- the calmness of a well-rested teacher

- the precision of a technical manual

- the consistency of a patient mentor

No individual human can maintain this level of clarity for hours at a time. The model maintains it automatically.

Not because it is intelligent. Because its training distribution captured humanity's most intelligent moments — and training smooths away the rest.

## The Paradox Resolved

This is why a prediction engine sounds smart:

- It learns from humanity's brightest material.

- It blends knowledge across domains effortlessly.

- Its predictions follow the statistical shape of reasoning.

- It removes emotional and structural noise.

- It expresses clarity with perfect stamina.

- It is incapable of sounding tired, rushed, or overwhelmed.

It is not smarter than humans. It is sampling from the smartest patterns of human writing and projecting them back with inhuman consistency.

## Why LLMs Outperform Humans in Consistency and Stamina

Humans are inconsistent thinkers.

Our clarity rises and falls with sleep, mood, stress, frustration, distractions, and physical condition. Cognitive fatigue degrades reasoning. Emotional triggers distort explanations. Under pressure, structure collapses.

A model does not degrade.

It outputs the same quality at midnight as at noon.

It never loses patience.

It never forgets the prior sentence.

It never becomes unfocused.

This perfect composure presents as intelligence — but it is merely the absence of human cognitive limits. Humans can maintain near-peak clarity for brief moments. A model can maintain it indefinitely.

That consistency alone creates an enormous perceived intelligence gap.

## Why LLMs Still Fail Despite Sounding Intelligent

For all their strengths, LLMs have real structural limitations:

- They cannot verify facts — only predict plausible ones.

- They cannot detect missing context — they fill gaps blindly.

- They cannot ground meaning — they map words to words, not to reality.

- They cannot reason about truth — only about patterns.

- They fail suddenly at the edges — inventing nonsense with confidence.

This is why human oversight is irreplaceable.

The machine provides fluency; the human provides judgment.

The system is not dangerous because it is too intelligent. It is dangerous because it sounds intelligent even when it is wrong.

Understanding this dual nature — brilliance in pattern, blindness in truth — is key to responsible deployment.

A language model does not represent a new mind. It represents a new mirror — polished by data, shaped by probability, reflecting the brightest and most coherent fragments of human thought back to us. Its intelligence is not its own; it is borrowed from us, amplified through scale, and delivered with flawless consistency.

The real opportunity is not replacing human judgment, but augmenting it.

Used wisely, this mirror becomes a tool that multiplies our ability to think, explain, design, and decide.

Used blindly, it becomes a confident voice without understanding.

In the chapters ahead, we turn from capability to responsibility: how to design workflows, oversight, and governance that keep the human firmly in the loop — where it belongs.

# Chapter 8 — Probabilities, Not Truths

Every AI output rests on a foundation of probability. Beneath each fluent paragraph or confident chart lies a ranked list of possible next words, each chosen according to its statistical likelihood. The model does not declare truth; it produces **the most probable continuation** of the patterns it has seen. When you ask, "Will revenue grow next quarter?" and the model replies, "Yes, by 5%," the answer is not revelation. It is a probabilistic echo — a statistically consistent guess shaped by the language of past financial analyses.

But not all AI tasks are probabilistic. Some are **deterministic**. When you hand the model a clean Excel table and ask, "How many rows have a date of January 5th?", it is not predicting — it is performing a direct logical operation. No creativity, no ambiguity, no statistical inference. Just reading, filtering, counting. Deterministic tasks let the model internally verify each step, which is why structured-data questions often feel 100% accurate even though other domains remain uncertain. **Prediction is probabilistic; computation is deterministic. Confusing the two is where errors — and misplaced trust — begin.**

This distinction also explains why scaffolding matters. Scaffolding is the deliberate act of structuring the model's reasoning: planning steps, retrieving data, verifying results, and only then generating an answer. The model itself doesn't suddenly gain intelligence — the workflow around it does. Scaffolding transforms a free-form probabilistic generator into something that behaves more like a process: predictable, inspectable, and auditable.

For organizations, scaffolding is governance in motion. A recruiting team might let AI screen résumés but require human review before decisions. A finance team might automate variance analysis while routing anomalies to managers. A compliance group might use AI to summarize regulations but require citations from verified sources. Scaffolding does not slow teams down; it scales accountability by ensuring that automation happens within defined boundaries.

A helpful mental model: **every domain has a confidence band —** a range of typical accuracy you can expect even from well-tuned enterprise-grade LLMs. These bands are not guarantees; they are directional averages under controlled conditions such as grounding, retrieval, or tool use:

| Domain | Typical Reliability (well-tuned model) |
| --- | --- |
| Math / Science | 95–99% |
| Factual recall | 90–95% |
| Logical reasoning | 75–85% |
| Causal inference | 60–80% |
| Forecasting | 50–70% |

These ranges describe **entire families of tasks,** not the simple, deterministic cases within them. Counting rows in Excel sits at the far right edge of the math band — essentially a guaranteed operation. Multi-step word problems sit at the lower end. Knowing where your task sits inside the band is what turns accuracy from a mystery into a management decision. This also shapes how you tune the model. Temperature and randomness allow you to trade creativity for certainty.

- **Lower temperature** → safer, more consistent output.

- **Higher temperature** → broader and creative variation.

The right setting depends not on what is possible, but on what is acceptable. Drafting marketing copy tolerates 80% accuracy. Drafting policy language demands 99%. Responsible AI is less about maximizing output and more about matching uncertainty to context.

Consider a logistics team forecasting shipment delays. Initial accuracy: 68%. After adding structured inputs — weather data, congestion indexes, real-time port conditions — and lowering the temperature to reduce randomness, accuracy climbs to 88%. The model has not "become smarter"; it has **narrowed uncertainty** by replacing guesswork with grounded data.

Probabilities invite humility. They remind us that intelligence — human or artificial — exists on a spectrum between guessing and knowing. The most responsible use of AI is not to replace judgment, but to quantify uncertainty so that judgment can focus where it matters. In risk management, that discipline is called calibration. In leadership, it is called awareness.

And the most important question to introduce into every meeting is the simplest one: **"How sure is it?"** Because behind every confident sentence from a model lies a probability curve — and the future of responsible AI depends on reading that curve correctly.

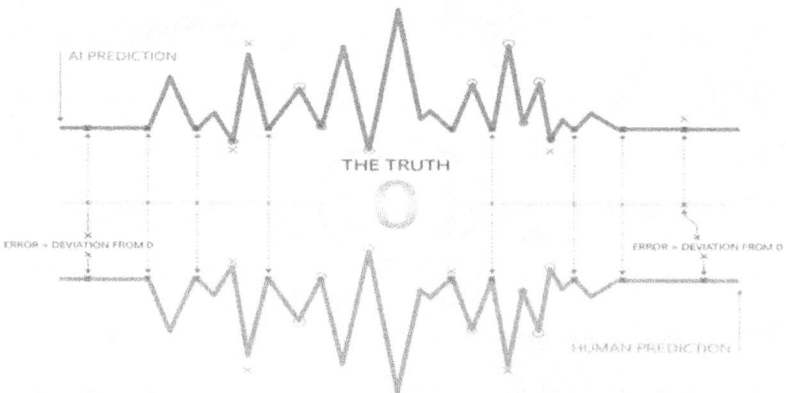

# Chapter 9 — The Epistemology of AI

Every system of intelligence, natural or artificial, lives under an invisible law: it can only act on what it believes to be true. Epistemology — the study of how we know what we know — asks a question most machines never get to ask: *What makes a belief justified?*

Humans acquire knowledge through experience, reflection, and dialogue. Machines acquire it through data, pattern, and probability. Both generate "truths," but only one can doubt them.

When a person says, "I know," they imply the capacity to be wrong. When a model outputs, "The answer is," it implies only correlation. The difference is humility. Epistemology is, in a sense, the **science of humility** — the recognition that knowing requires questioning.

## Knowledge Without Experience

A machine's "knowledge" is statistical: it knows that certain words or events often occur together. It cannot distinguish between *true but rare* and *false but frequent*. Humans can — not always well, but often enough to notice the tension between fact and familiarity.

Epistemic maturity means asking not only *what is probable* but *what is reliable*.

In organizations, this distinction matters deeply. Predictive dashboards can model risk, but only experience interprets it. A model may say, "98% confidence," but epistemology reminds us to ask, "98% of what kind of knowledge?"

## The Architecture of Knowing

Philosophers traditionally describe knowledge as a three-part structure:
**Justified True Belief.**

| Component | Human Form | AI Analogy | Failure |
|-----------|------------|------------|---------|
| **Belief** | Conviction or hypothesis | Model output | Overfitting |
| **Truth** | Reality correspondence | Ground truth data | Data drift |
| **Justification** | Evidence or reasoning | Training or retrieval | Hallucination |

Machines excel at belief and partial truth, but lack self-aware justification. They output probabilities without provenance — confident, consistent, context-blind.

## The Three Pillars of Knowledge

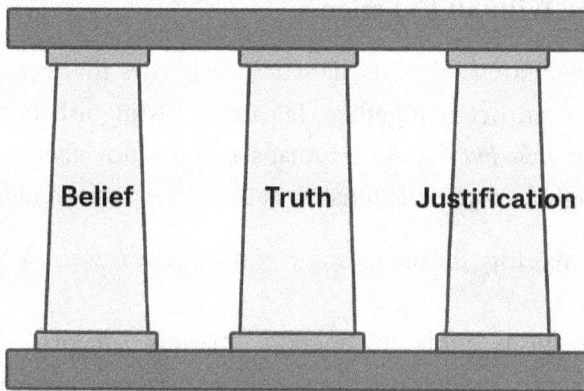

Belief          Truth          Justification

- Belief must correspond to reality.
- Justification lends confidence to belief.

Humans, for all our flaws, evolved the reverse habit: uncertainty first, justification second, belief last. In that sequence lies responsibility.

## Knowing vs. Predicting

Epistemology reveals the quiet divide between *intelligence* and *awareness*.

To predict is to extend the past; to know is to test it. Prediction follows the curve of correlation; knowledge resists it when new evidence appears.

That resistance — the ability to say, "I was wrong" — is not a weakness; it's the root of cognition. If machines ever develop wisdom, it will begin not with faster prediction, but with the first genuine hesitation.


A system that cannot question its own certainty will always confuse fluency with truth. Epistemology doesn't slow progress; it keeps meaning attached to it. Before asking what machines will know next, we might first ask what they are capable of *believing*.

## Closing Reflection — Part II: Inside the Synthetic Mind

Language models don't think in sentences; they think in geometry. Meaning becomes distance, probability becomes gravity. Once you see it that way, you stop expecting understanding and start engineering context.

The lesson of this section is simple: precision doesn't come from bigger models, but from better boundaries. Grounding, scaffolding, and retrieval aren't accessories — they are ethics expressed as architecture.

In the next part, we confront what happens when those boundaries fail — when confident correlation masquerades as reason.

# PART III — THE MIRAGE OF THOUGHT

## Chapter 10 — Hallucination: When Correlation Lies

If prediction is the engine of artificial intelligence, hallucination is its exhaust. It is what escapes when probability outruns truth. A model hallucinates when it generates content that fits its learned patterns but lacks real-world support. Ask a chatbot for a citation, and it may invent one. Ask it for a timeline of events, and it may merge two decades into one narrative. The model is not lying; it is completing a pattern where a blank appeared. The temptation is to blame the machine. Yet hallucination mirrors a human habit: filling gaps with plausible stories. When we misremember a conversation or embellish a résumé, we too create pattern-consistent fiction. The machine merely does it faster and with better grammar.

**Why it happens.** Inside the model, every next word is chosen from a probability field. If "Harvard Business Review" often follows discussions of management, the model will summon that phrase whether or not the article exists. The pattern dominates the proof. In a sense, the model is doing exactly what it was built to do — predict coherence, not confirm reality.

**Why it matters.** In low-stakes contexts — drafting marketing copy, brainstorming titles, writing internal summaries — hallucination is tolerable. In regulated industries, it's toxic. A single fabricated medical reference can breach compliance; a phantom legal clause can mislead a client. In corporate settings, even small hallucinations can cascade — a made-up quote in a briefing, a false figure in a report, or an incorrect citation in a client deliverable can quietly erode trust.

**How to manage it.**

1. **Add context.** Feed the model reference material before generation.

2. **Constrain outputs.** Specify format and permissible sources.

3. **Require citation.** Force evidence with retrievers or databases.

4. **Escalate review.** Route high-impact results to human oversight.

Imagine a legal team using an AI model to summarize case law. Early drafts include fictional precedents that sound perfectly authentic. After adding a retrieval layer that pulls only from a verified legal database, hallucinations drop by 92 %. The model didn't gain honesty; it gained context.

Across industries, the same principle holds: hallucination decreases when context increases. Customer-service bots improve when tied to live knowledge bases. Research assistants get safer when connected to document repositories. Strategy tools become reliable only when their data sources are named, current, and traceable.

Think of hallucination like optical illusion. A straight stick looks bent in water until you change your viewing medium. Likewise, prediction looks truthful until you change its medium to verification. The issue isn't that AI imagines; it's that we often stop checking what it imagines *against*.

The lesson for professionals is simple: treat every fluent answer as a draft of probability, not a statement of fact. Hallucination is not a glitch — it's a reminder that language can be convincing even when it is wrong. Trust in AI begins not with belief, but with the discipline to verify.

# Chapter 11 — X ÷ 0 and the Limits of Logic

There is a certain beauty in mathematics: rules so precise they cannot bend. Yet that rigidity also exposes fragility. Try dividing any number by zero and logic collapses — not because the number misbehaved, but because the framework broke down.

AI faces similar boundaries. Models excel at *interpolation* — filling the space between known examples. What they cannot do is reason beyond those bounds without guidance. Asking a model to infer a principle it has never statistically seen is like asking it to divide by zero: it will produce something undefined yet confident.

Take an everyday case. A predictive model trained on five years of consumer data forecasts next quarter's demand. Then a pandemic hits. The probability landscape shifts; yesterday's equations no longer apply. The model will still output numbers, but those numbers belong to a vanished world.

In business, this kind of failure happens quietly. A risk model keeps approving loans in an economy that no longer exists. A retention model keeps rewarding employees for pre-hybrid-work behaviors. A supply-chain optimizer keeps minimizing cost while ignoring suddenly priceless resilience. Each is a digital version of dividing by zero — the data space it relies on has collapsed.

Undefined does not mean useless. It means *stop and reframe*. When your ratios explode or vanish, the anomaly itself is information. It tells you that your assumptions are outdated, your data incomplete, or your causal structure missing. In analytics, an undefined result is often the first honest signal that something truly new is happening.

In organizational terms:

• **When dashboards spike inexplicably, pause automation.** Don't retrain the model before you understand the cause.

• **When patterns break, revisit inputs before redesigning outputs.** Garbage in, governance out.

• **When the system insists on certainty, ask for its evidence.** A confident answer without context is a calculation without denominator.

Human reasoning benefits from ambiguity tolerance; we know when we don't know. Machines need that humility engineered into them. Guardrails, thresholds, and *out-of-distribution* detectors play the role of mathematicians saying, "Division by zero — stop." In plain terms, these are circuit-breakers that catch inputs too different from anything the model has seen before.

One engineering team added such detectors to a credit-risk model. Whenever a customer's profile fell outside the training range, the system withheld prediction and flagged the case for manual review. Accuracy rose, but more importantly, trust rose. People respected a model that admitted, *"I can't calculate that."*

The lesson scales upward. Strategic forecasting tools, fraud-detection systems, even AI copilots for management reports all need the same humility. Logic is powerful precisely because it breaks loudly when limits are reached. Good AI systems should do the same.

Undefined is not failure; it is feedback. Knowing when to stop predicting is itself a higher form of intelligence — the kind that turns automation into awareness.

# Chapter 12 — Prompting the Machine

If training builds the model's mind, prompting is how we speak to it.

Every organization has learned that technology amplifies the quality of its questions. AI makes that truth unavoidable. The prompt is no longer a technical instruction — it's a managerial act of framing: defining purpose, boundaries, and tone in a single line.

We live in a time where attention is the rarest currency. Everyone is busy, distracted, half-listening. AI quietly solves part of that problem — not by giving you answers, but by being the only companion that never gets tired of your questions. Yet it also exposes a new truth: the value is not in asking many questions, but in asking the *right* ones.

The most powerful queries are the ones most people avoid — the uncomfortable, high-risk questions: *What are we missing? What could fail? What don't we want to measure?* The rarest questions in AI are not about capability but about *consequence*. A prompt is not a casual instruction; it's a specification document compressed into a sentence.

Every strong interaction follows six elements: **Background, Goal, Input, Output, Constraints, Tone/Audience.** Neglect any one, and ambiguity multiplies.

For example, compare these two prompts:

1. "Write a summary of our Q2 sales report."

2. "Background: Q2 sales report in attached text. Goal: Provide 200-word summary highlighting regional trends. Output: Structured bullets for executive slide. Tone: Professional."

The second yields consistent results because it mirrors a work order. You wouldn't hand a contractor a one-word brief; don't hand an AI one either.

Prompting also means thinking like a systems designer:

- **Temperature** controls randomness — creativity versus precision.

- **Top-p** sets how much of the probability pool is considered — it limits the model to the most likely words until their combined probability reaches that threshold.

- **Max tokens** limits verbosity — it caps how many words the model can generate before stopping.

- **Role instructions** define persona ("Act as a compliance officer...").

In teams, prompting becomes a new literacy. Early adopters often create *prompt libraries* — collections of reusable templates for recurring tasks such as summarization, policy drafting, or data interpretation. These are the modern equivalent of macros. Standardizing them turns experimentation into a repeatable process.

## From Prompt to Dialogue to Template

Most great prompts don't start great — they *become* great. You begin with a rough instruction, see the result, then tweak it again and again until the outcome matches your intention. By the time you get the result you want, your "prompt" has evolved into a conversation. The art lies in distilling that conversation back into a single reusable instruction.

To do that, retrace your edits. Every correction you gave the model — "shorter," "more formal," "add examples" — reveals what your real intent was. Convert each piece of feedback into a clear rule:

*"under 200 words," "include numbered steps," "for executive audience."* Then rebuild it as one structured prompt:

**Background → Goal → Output → Tone → Constraints.**

A good prompt isn't discovered; it's designed. Your best future prompts are born from your best past conversations.

There's psychology too. The machine mirrors your tone. Ask politely and clearly, and it behaves predictably; feed sarcasm or contradiction, and it reflects noise. In essence, the model is a probability echo of your own precision. A supervision manager once joked that prompting felt like teaching manners to a brilliant but literal intern with one-day memory. That's accurate — examples and boundaries train style as much as substance.

For complex tasks, pair prompting with retrieval or external logic. Generation alone is like brainstorming; generation plus data access becomes research. The more grounded your inputs, the less cleanup later.

Over time, teams that master prompting evolve faster. They move from reacting to AI surprises to *designing* AI behavior. They stop thinking of prompts as hacks and start treating them as strategy.

Prompting is not magic words — it's disciplined communication. It is to AI what leadership memos were to organizations: short, clear, directional, and consequential. And as with all communication, clarity is kindness.

# Closing Reflection — Part III: The Mirage of Thought

Every illusion of intelligence hides a mirror of ourselves. When a model hallucinates, it exposes our appetite for certainty. When it improvises, it reveals how often we do the same.

The purpose of this part wasn't to condemn the machine, but to remind us that its flaws are familiar. Bias, overconfidence, selective memory — they are human traits rendered statistical.

The path forward is not to silence prediction, but to supervise it. Next, we turn from diagnosis to design — from what fails to how to build systems that know their limits.

# PART IV — BEYOND THE ILLUSION

## Chapter 13 – Grounding: The Missing Sense of Reality

A child learns that words point to things. "Apple" isn't just sound — it's the red object in front of them, tangible and sweet.

Large language models never had that childhood. They learn words from other words, not from apples. This is the core of the *grounding problem*: AI systems generate fluent language but have no built-in connection to the physical or factual world. They can describe "the taste of an apple" with poetic precision without ever having one roll across their metaphorical desk.

In organizations, this disconnect shows up daily. A model writes a confident market summary that references a "trend" no analyst has seen. A chatbot cites an article that doesn't exist. A data assistant answers a financial query with authority — and without verification. The illusion isn't malevolent; it's mechanical. The model knows how sentences should sound, not how facts should stand.

**Grounding means giving machines a sense of reality.** It's the difference between describing gravity and dropping a ball. Without grounding, an AI can predict what an answer *should* look like but cannot verify whether it's true.

There are three main forms of grounding in practice:

1. **Data grounding** — linking outputs to verifiable sources (retrieval-augmented generation, database queries).

58

2. **Tool grounding** — allowing the model to perform actions that test its own statements (calculators, APIs, code interpreters).

3. **Human grounding** — closing the loop with review, judgment, or feedback.

When all three combine, probability becomes evidence.

Take a corporate scenario. A financial analyst asks a model to project next quarter's revenue. Without grounding, it invents a number consistent with linguistic patterns — 4.3 %, say. With grounding, it pulls the latest actuals from an internal data warehouse, applies a simple regression script, and explains the reasoning behind the 4.3 %. Same output, different ontology: one is guess, the other derivation.

Grounding changes behavior in subtle ways. It discourages confident fabrication and encourages transparency. A grounded system can answer, *"I don't have recent data for that,"* instead of guessing. For decision-makers, that humility is gold.

Each grounding layer plays a different role in governance:

- **Data grounding** builds audit trails — it makes every claim traceable.

- **Tool grounding** builds functional trust — it lets the model check itself before others do.

- **Human grounding** builds cultural trust — it reminds organizations that oversight is not a flaw but a feature.

Analogies help. Think of grounding as a model's GPS. Without it, language is free-floating — like directions shouted by someone who's never been to the city. With it, the model knows the map, the coordinates, and when to stop talking.

The near future of AI will depend less on making models bigger and more on grounding them better — connecting their eloquence to the world they describe. This is where enterprise value lives: not in raw generation, but in verified generation.

When you design or buy AI tools, ask three questions:
• **What sources can it verify against?**

• **What tools can it use to test itself?**

• **Who checks its work?**

Grounding doesn't just make machines more accurate; it makes humans more accountable. It turns prediction into procedure and language into evidence. When organizations adopt grounding as a governance principle, AI becomes not just a storyteller — but a reliable partner in truth.

# Chapter 14 – The Human Mirror

Every time you ask an AI a question, it quietly studies the way you ask.

Language models learn from us — not only our facts but our habits of thought. They mirror back the reasoning shortcuts, the biases, the optimism, and the anxiety embedded in our text. In many ways, they don't just process our language; they process our worldview.

Daniel Kahneman described two modes of human thinking: **System 1**, fast and intuitive; and **System 2**, slow and deliberate. AI systems overwhelmingly resemble System 1 — quick association, pattern completion, confident continuity. What they lack is System 2: reflection, self-critique, and the ability to question their own first answer.

When organizations treat model output as gospel, they effectively promote System 1 to CEO. The result is efficient error — decisions made at the speed of intuition, without the pause of reflection.

To restore balance, pair the model's speed with human deliberation:
• Use AI for **proposal generation**, not final verdicts.

• Combine outputs with **rule-based checks or governance scripts** that catch inconsistencies.

• Encourage teams to **label responses** as draft, verified, or pending review — small language cues that preserve responsibility.

These practices turn speed into structure. They slow thinking down just enough to let judgment in. In effect, they re-introduce System 2 into digital workflows — the deliberate mind supervising the automatic one.

The mirror metaphor carries ethical weight. If a model produces biased or superficial answers, it reflects the data we gave it —

historical hiring patterns, cultural stereotypes, linguistic imbalances. Blaming the mirror does nothing; cleaning the room does.

Consider recruitment algorithms that favored male candidates because historical data equated "success" with male-dominated résumés. The fix wasn't moral pleading but **data redesign**: balancing examples, re-weighting features, inserting human review points. The same principle applies in finance, healthcare, and marketing — wherever predictive systems learn from imperfect histories.

For individuals, the mirror invites humility. When you see a model produce brilliant insight followed by nonsense, remember that both came from our collective corpus. The brilliance is ours — and so is the noise. AI doesn't invent our contradictions; it illuminates them.

In this sense, AI is not replacing us — it's *exposing* us. It holds a magnifying glass to the structures of reasoning we take for granted, showing how much of human thought is statistical habit. If we use that reflection well, it becomes diagnostic rather than dangerous.

The smartest organizations will treat models as cognitive mirrors: tools for seeing how their teams think, decide, and communicate. They'll analyze which questions employees ask the model, what biases appear in its drafts, and where reflection vanishes under routine.

The goal isn't to automate the mind but to audit it — to see, perhaps for the first time, how human thinking itself can be optimized not by machines, but through the clarity machines provide.

# Chapter 15 – Beyond Prediction

After enough conversations with machines, a pattern emerges: the most valuable answers are not the ones that sound human but the ones that **make humans think**.

Prediction can take us only so far. It describes what is likely, not what ought to be. AI does not turn us into robots; failing to verify its output does. The risk isn't that machines will replace human judgment — it's that we'll stop exercising it. When people copy-and-paste AI answers without questioning, adjusting, or adding their own context, the work becomes mechanized, not the workers. The solution isn't resisting AI, but engaging with it critically: refining its drafts, challenging its assumptions, and layering in the human nuance the system can never generate on its own. Automation doesn't erase humanity; uncritical dependence does.

To move beyond prediction is to reintroduce intent — purpose, accountability, and causation. In other words, it's to restore leadership to the loop.

Modern AI excels at pattern completion but struggles with causal reasoning. It can tell you that markets with rising interest rates often experience slower lending, but it cannot tell you *why* unless explicitly modeled. The "why" requires theory, context, and values — all human territory.

Causal reasoning is what allows us to distinguish *correlation* from *consequence*. In business, it's the difference between seeing that customer churn rises after price increases and understanding that it rises only when service quality drops first. Machines detect association; people detect intention.

The future of intelligent systems will blend three elements:

1. **Grounding** — connecting language to verified data.

2. **Memory** — allowing systems to learn from ongoing interaction instead of each session starting from zero.

3. **Causal learning** — training models not just on correlation but on interventions and outcomes.

Together, these move us closer to tools that understand in a functional sense — systems that can simulate experiments, test assumptions, and explain failure.

Yet even then, human oversight remains the keystone. Prediction without ethics becomes exploitation; automation without judgment becomes drift.

There's a growing misconception that when an outcome involves AI, responsibility somehow transfers to the machine. But tools don't own outcomes — people do. We don't credit Excel for building a dashboard, or PowerPoint for persuading a client. We credit the analyst or manager who used them with judgment. The same logic applies to AI.

A model can draft, summarize, simulate, or score — but the act of *deciding* remains human. It's easy to say "the AI did it," but that's like blaming the calculator for the tax return. What matters is not whether a system generated the words or numbers, but whether the human using it understood, reviewed, and owned them. AI doesn't replace agency; it tests it.

Consider aviation. Autopilot systems predict flight stability every millisecond, but pilots remain in the cockpit for the moments prediction cannot foresee — weather anomalies, sensor faults, moral decisions about risk. The same principle applies to organizational AI: **automation everywhere, abdication nowhere.**

To operate beyond prediction is to design collaboration:

• Machines surface probabilities; humans apply principles.

• Machines compress knowledge; humans assign meaning.

• Machines optimize; humans contextualize.

This partnership is not science fiction — it's management science. Companies that treat AI as *colleague* rather than *oracle* will outperform those that chase headlines. They will measure success not by "AI adoption rate" but by error reduction, decision transparency, and human bandwidth reclaimed.

To go beyond prediction is to ask a deeper question — not "What can AI do?" but "What should we do with it?" The phrase *Beyond Prediction* is therefore more than a title; it is a compass. It challenges us to build systems that think responsibly — and to build organizations wise enough to guide them.

# Closing Reflection — Part IV: Beyond the Illusion

Theory ends where process begins. Grounding, scaffolding, and governance only matter when they shape actual workflows. The responsible organization doesn't wait for policy; it prototypes ethics daily.

This part marked the turning point — from philosophy to practice. In the chapters ahead, we'll see how responsible systems are built, monitored, and improved, one decision at a time.

# PART V — OPERATIONS AND GOVERNANCE

## Chapter 16 – Key Takeaways for Professionals

### The Art of Simplicity

One of my professors in nuclear engineering once explained a complex reactor process as if he were describing how to boil water. No formulas, no diagrams — just calm clarity. At that moment I realized something important: **the people who understand complexity best are the ones who can explain it simply.**

Data, like physics, hides its truths behind layers of precision. The temptation — especially in professional settings — is to sound sophisticated rather than to seek understanding. Yet the deeper your technical literacy becomes, the more humility you acquire about how fragile comprehension really is.

In analytics and AI, simplicity isn't a lack of depth; it's the final stage of mastery. A professional who truly understands data can translate it into plain language — the "why" behind the numbers, not just the numbers themselves.

Before you let a model analyze your data, **you must first understand what the data means.** Otherwise, automation becomes imitation: numbers speaking without context. Professionals who ground their insights in meaning — who know what a variable represents, what an outlier implies, what a ratio hides — can use AI responsibly. Those who skip that understanding risk producing elegant nonsense faster than ever.

It is easy to ask a machine to find patterns; it is harder to ask the *right* question. The discipline of clarity — knowing your inputs, articulating your assumptions, and keeping explanations simple enough to teach — is not a style choice. It is the essence of responsible intelligence.

Simplicity is not the opposite of sophistication. It is its proof.

After dozens of pages and thousands of words, it's time to step back. What does all this mean in practice — for leaders, analysts, project managers, or anyone steering a modern organization through an era of predictive machines?

AI is not a monolith; it's an ecosystem of tools that convert data into decisions. Mastery lies not in knowing every algorithm but in designing how you use them. The following ten principles summarize the mental model that separates effective adopters from reckless enthusiasts.

1. **Define tasks narrowly.**

   "AI for marketing" is too broad. "Generate first-draft email subject lines tested for tone" is manageable. Narrow scopes reduce noise and make results measurable.

2. **Ground every output.**

   Treat grounding as the oxygen of accuracy. Connect models to retrievers, databases, or rule engines before trusting what they say.

3. **Constrain formats.**

   Decide whether the answer should be a paragraph, a table, or JSON. Structure limits hallucination; unstructured text invites fantasy.

4. **Tune randomness deliberately.**

   Low temperature for compliance and analysis, medium for summarization, high for ideation. Don't rely on defaults; tune by intention.

5. **Add retrieval.**

   Before generation, feed facts. In human terms: read before you write. Retrieval converts storytelling into reporting.

6. **Validate claims.**

   Every confident sentence deserves a fact-check. Build feedback loops — peer review, secondary models, or audit scripts — that test truth rather than tone.

7. **Track errors.**

   Don't just celebrate success cases. Classify failures: fabrication, omission, bias, logic drift. Over time, this taxonomy becomes institutional memory.

8. **Document assumptions.**

   If a model relies on 2023 data or a specific prompt template, record it. Tomorrow's post-mortem depends on today's transparency.

9. **Keep humans in the loop.**

   Automation without oversight creates fragility. Assign responsibility clearly: who approves, who monitors, who explains when outputs go wrong.

10. **Treat models as coworkers, not oracles.**

    Colleagues can assist, surprise, and occasionally err. You supervise them; you don't worship them.

Applied together, these principles form a management discipline — **AI Ops for thought.** The goal is not blind efficiency but calibrated trust: systems that extend human capability while preserving accountability.

To test whether your organization is mature in its AI usage, ask three diagnostic questions:

• Do we know where our data comes from?

• Do we know what our models are trained to ignore?

• Do we know who is responsible for verifying outputs?

If you can answer all three without hesitation, you're not just using AI; you're *governing* it.

The business advantage of such maturity is enormous. Teams waste less time cleaning hallucinated data, leaders gain clearer visibility, and clients see fewer surprises. AI doesn't replace competence — it amplifies it. The organizations that thrive will be those that remember that amplification multiplies both clarity and confusion. The difference lies in management.

# Chapter 17 – Why This Book Matters

The story of artificial intelligence is really the story of human aspiration.

Every generation invents tools that mirror how it thinks. The abacus counted, the computer calculated, and the modern model converses. Each stage brought a new form of assistance — from tallying numbers to reasoning with words. But the deeper question isn't what it can do; it's what we choose to do with it.

This book matters because prediction has become invisible. Every recommendation algorithm, fraud detector, translation app, and chatbot in your life is quietly forecasting what comes next. The world now runs on probabilistic sentences. Understanding that reality is as vital today as financial literacy once was.

For decision-makers, the new literacy includes three abilities:

1. **Interpret probabilistic output.** Don't ask, *"Is it right?"* — ask, *"How sure is it, and on what basis?"*

2. **Design human + machine workflows.** Know when to delegate to code and when to escalate to conscience. Some tasks should be handled by automation, but others require human moral or ethical judgment — decisions where empathy, fairness, or responsibility matter.

3. **Explain outcomes transparently.** Accountability is not optional; it's a competitive advantage.

This book also matters as a cultural mirror. AI systems have exposed how much of human communication is statistical habit — phrases repeated until they sound like truth. By studying the machine, we rediscover our own shortcuts. We remember that reasoning takes effort and that explanation is an act of leadership.

If there's one closing argument, it's this: **Ambition must meet discipline.**

The organizations that balance those forces will use AI not just to automate but to illuminate — to reveal inefficiencies, biases, and blind spots that once hid behind complexity.

Corporate history suggests that every tool meant to "save time" eventually creates a new meeting. AI might break that cycle — or just automate the calendar invites faster.

You, the reader, now possess that lens. Use it. Build workflows where prediction serves purpose. Speak about AI precisely, implement it cautiously, and demand from it the same rigor you demand from people.

The future of intelligence — artificial or otherwise — depends less on new algorithms and more on wiser operators. Let that be the legacy of your generation of leaders: not just smarter machines, but saner ones.

# Chapter 18 — The Human in the Loop: Designing Responsible Systems

Modern organizations have learned that no single model, however advanced, is intelligent on its own. True intelligence emerges from the combination of model, workflow, and oversight — a choreography of prediction, verification, and decision.

AI systems do not operate in isolation; they live inside processes. A fraud-detection algorithm influences credit decisions. A résumé screener shapes hiring outcomes. A forecasting model guides budget allocations. Each becomes part of a chain — and every link in that chain determines whether the result is responsible or reckless.

The most effective companies no longer ask, *"Can the model do this?"* They ask, *"Should the model do this — and who checks when it does?"* That mindset shift marks the beginning of responsible design.

**The Governance Pyramid:** A Framework for Responsible AI

The Governance Pyramid is a conceptual model illustrating the three essential, tiered layers required for building and deploying responsible, trustworthy, and auditable AI systems. Each layer supports the one above it, emphasizing that a solid foundation is crucial for effective governance at the top.

# GOVERNANCE PYRAMID

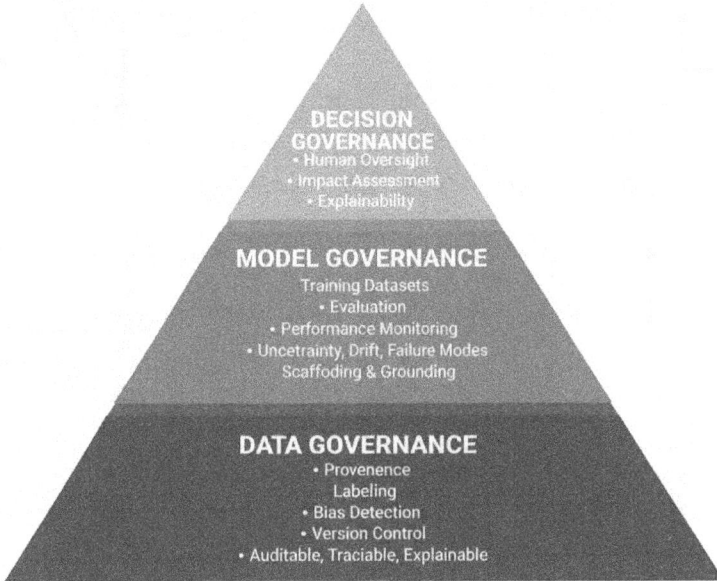

**DECISION
GOVERNANCE**
• Human Oversight
• Impact Assessment
• Explainability

**MODEL GOVERNANCE**
Training Datasets
• Evaluation
• Performance Monitoring
• Uncetrainty, Drift, Failure Modes
Scaffoding & Grounding

**DATA GOVERNANCE**
• Provenence
Labeling
• Bias Detection
• Version Control
• Auditable, Traciable, Explainable

## Base: Data Governance

This is the foundational layer and the most critical element for trust. Every responsible system begins with data discipline.

- Core Principle: If the input is opaque, the output cannot be trusted.

- Key Responsibilities:

  o Clear Provenance: Knowing the source, history, and modifications of all data.

  o Consistent Labeling: Standardized and accurate annotation of data.

- o Bias Detection: Proactively identifying and mitigating hidden or systemic biases in the datasets.

- o Version Control: Maintaining auditable records of data versions used for training specific models.

- Outcome: Organizations that treat data as an asset class—auditable, traceable, and explainable—discover that model governance becomes easier by design.

## Middle: Model Governance

This layer builds upon disciplined data to ensure the integrity and accountability of the AI models themselves. Here lies the structure of accountability.

- Core Principle: Good models declare their limits.

- Key Responsibilities:

  - o Documented Training Datasets: Clear records of the exact data used for training and testing.

  - o Evaluation Benchmarks: Established metrics and tests for assessing model quality before deployment.

  - o Performance Monitoring: Continuous tracking of model behavior in the wild (e.g., accuracy, fairness metrics).

  - o Logging: Documenting uncertainty, drift (degradation in predictive power), and known failure modes.

- Practical Application: This is where techniques like scaffolding and grounding move from concept to practice, ensuring models operate within defined guardrails.

## Top: Decision Governance

This is the highest and often overlooked layer. It addresses how the organization uses the AI model's outputs in real-world processes.

- Core Principle: This layer ensures that the output of a governed model is used responsibly and ethically in human-centric decision-making systems.

- Key Responsibilities:

    o Defining Human Oversight: When and how a human reviews or overrides an AI-driven decision.

    o Impact Assessment: Analyzing the societal, ethical, and business impact of AI-driven decisions.

    o Explainability to End-Users: Ensuring stakeholders can understand why a model made a specific recommendation.

A prediction means nothing until it meets a decision. Who approves? Who monitors? Who explains? Decision governance defines these thresholds — ensuring that human judgment remains the final checkpoint.

Together, these layers form the architecture of trust. Without the base, models drift. Without the middle, bias spreads. Without the top, accountability disappears.

## Design Patterns Across Industries

**Finance:**
Banks now build "human-in-the-loop" validation cells — teams that review flagged transactions and retrain models on edge cases. Their goal isn't perfection but traceability. Every false positive becomes training data; every escalation, a governance log.

**Healthcare:**

Hospitals deploying diagnostic AI require double sign-off — algorithmic score plus clinician judgment. The model accelerates detection, but only licensed professionals interpret results. This dual-loop design prevents automation bias — the tendency to trust the screen more than the patient.

**Human Resources:**

Recruitment algorithms are audited for demographic drift. Whenever model predictions start correlating with protected attributes (gender, race, age), human review pauses automation. Fairness isn't statistical — it's procedural.

**From Compliance to Culture**

The ultimate goal of responsible AI isn't merely avoiding penalties; it's building credibility. Organizations with transparent oversight don't just meet regulations — they earn trust. When employees see accountability modeled in code and policy, responsibility scales naturally.

In the age of prediction, leadership means designing systems that deserve belief.

# Closing Reflection — Part V: Practice and Governance

Governance isn't bureaucracy; it's choreography. It aligns data, models, and judgment into a repeatable rhythm of accountability. When done right, it turns trust from a slogan into a system.

But governance is not the destination. Beyond process lies purpose. The final part of this book looks outward — at work, education, and society — asking what kind of civilization emerges when prediction becomes ordinary.

# Part VI — New Horizons

## Chapter 19 — The Future of Work and Learning

Technology changes faster than human habits. Every generation of tools reshapes what it means to be competent. AI will do the same — not by erasing jobs, but by redefining what "thinking work" looks like.

### AI as Cognitive Infrastructure

Just as electricity became invisible infrastructure for power, AI is becoming infrastructure for cognition. It automates pattern recognition the way motors automated motion. Every spreadsheet, email client, and meeting note will soon contain a predictive layer — an ambient assistant suggesting, summarizing, and simulating.

The shift isn't from human to machine labor; it's from manual reasoning to supervised reasoning. Professionals will still think — but with an exoskeleton of prediction wrapped around them.

### New Literacies

Success in this new environment depends on literacies that schools rarely teach:

1.  Prompting as Specification. The ability to frame clear goals, constraints, and tone — transforming vague ideas into executable instructions.

2.  Data Framing. Understanding what information to feed a model, and what not to. Context discipline becomes a competitive edge.

3. Verification. The discipline of tracing claims back to sources. Future leaders will be judged less by speed of answers and more by rigor of validation.

These skills blend creativity with control — the dual mindset of the modern professional.

## Curiosity as Advantage

In a world saturated with automation, curiosity becomes differentiation.
AI is an endless sparring partner for thought — always ready, always responsive, never tired. The best thinkers will not use it for shortcuts but for stretching their reasoning. The quality of insight will depend on the quality of questions.

As attention grows scarce, curiosity becomes the rarest currency. The leaders who cultivate it — who stay in dialogue with their tools rather than delegating blindly — will remain irreplaceable.

## Learning Never Stops

Training programs will evolve from "skill acquisition" to "thinking augmentation."
Continuous learning means learning *with* machines, not *about* them. Workplaces that design AI-literate environments — open experimentation, shared prompt libraries, transparent review — will accelerate faster than those guarding old hierarchies.

The future belongs to the curious, the cautious, and the collaborative. They will not fear AI; they will teach it how to serve.

# Chapter 20 — Beyond Prediction in Society

Every technological revolution begins with fascination and ends with governance. The printing press democratized knowledge; electricity democratized power. AI is now democratizing reasoning — and with it, decision-making itself.

## The Paradox of Prediction

When everything predicts, responsibility blurs. If an algorithm scores credit, ranks candidates, or suggests medical paths, who decides the consequences? When we outsource judgment, we also outsource ethics.

This is the paradox of prediction: the more accurate systems become, the easier it is to forget they are probabilistic. Certainty becomes performance — confidence without conscience.

## The Governance Horizon

Society is entering a new social contract with technology. Transparency will replace secrecy as the measure of progress. The public will demand to know how decisions are made, not just that they work. This will reshape regulation, journalism, and education.

Ethical AI cannot rely solely on voluntary pledges. It requires traceable data supply chains, auditable algorithms, and enforceable standards for explainability. Regulation is not the enemy of innovation; it is the foundation of trust.

## The Historical Echo

Every revolution redefines agency. The printing press empowered readers; electricity empowered manufacturers; AI will empower interpreters — those who can translate between algorithm and society.

Future historians may look back and see this decade as the one when knowledge became negotiable — when humanity learned to manage its synthetic reflection.

## Letter to the Next Generation of Leaders

To the reader who leads tomorrow's institutions: remember that prediction is a tool, not a truth. It can simulate judgment but never replace it. The systems you design will inherit your values, not your intentions. Guard them well.

Build not just smarter machines, but wiser processes. The world doesn't need omniscience; it needs accountability. And when every dashboard glows with certainty, let your legacy be the quiet discipline of doubt.

# Closing Reflection — Part VI: New Horizons

Every generation inherits a frontier it does not fully understand. For ours, that frontier is not geography but cognition — the expanding boundary between what humans intend and what machines predict.

AI has become the new literacy of leadership. To work with it wisely is not to master code, but to master consequence: to know when to trust a pattern, when to question it, and when to stop asking the machine and start asking ourselves.

The story of prediction will continue, written in every prompt, dashboard, and decision. But its direction remains ours to choose. If the past taught us to automate, the future will teach us to interpret. And perhaps wisdom, in this new age, will mean what it always has — seeing clearly, acting carefully, and remembering that tools expand our reach only when they deepen our responsibility.

Beyond prediction lies intention. That is where the next chapter of intelligence will truly begin.

# EPILOGUE — THE EDGE OF UNDERSTANDING

When a system can predict perfectly yet still not know why, it mirrors the boundary of our own cognition. We, too, act on pattern and instinct more often than on full comprehension. The pursuit of AI therefore becomes a philosophical mirror: in teaching machines to reason, we confront how little of our reasoning is explicit.

The edge of understanding is not a cliff but a frontier. Every technological advance expands that frontier outward, forcing us to ask new questions about responsibility and meaning. What happens when our tools speak faster than we can verify? When forecasts feel truer than facts?

The answer is discipline. Not restraint out of fear, but structure out of respect — respect for complexity, for evidence, and for the limits that keep systems safe.

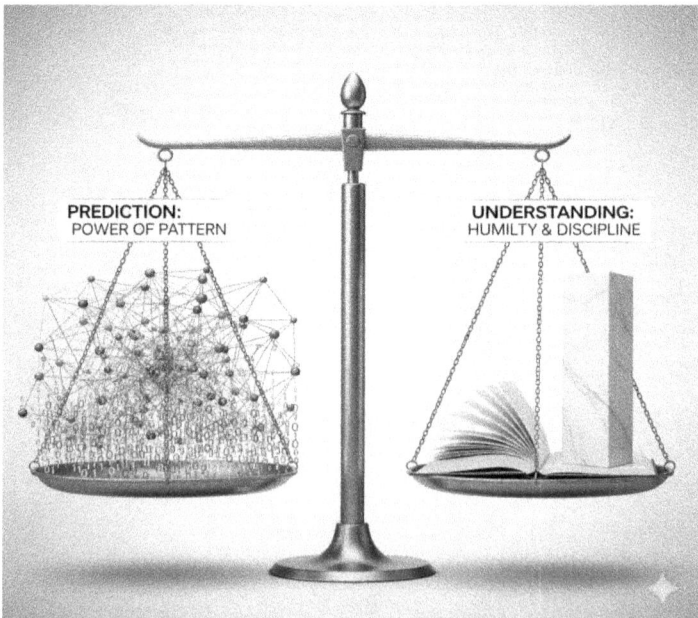

Prediction is easy. Understanding is hard. To live beyond prediction is to hold both truths: the power of pattern and the humility of ignorance.

Let this book be a small contribution to that balance — a guide for those building, buying, or governing the next generation of intelligence. The work begins not in machines but in minds willing to think a little slower, a little clearer, and a little further than yesterday.

# AFTERWORD — THE LAST HUMAN ADVANTAGE

As AI systems accelerate, the true differentiator will not be speed but *sense* — the human capacity to pause, reflect, and decide with care. This book began as an exploration of machines, but it ends as an invitation to humans: to think better, not just faster. In the end, intelligence may not be about speed, scale, or accuracy. It may be about restraint — the ability to stop predicting when the pattern becomes too painful to complete. We taught machines to finish our sentences, but somewhere along the way, they began finishing our silences too. The tragedy isn't that they speak — it's that we listen less to ourselves when they do.

Perhaps every age of progress carries a private loneliness. The printing press ended the village storyteller. Electricity ended the candle's ritual. AI, for all its brilliance, may end something smaller but dearer — the slow, unrecorded act of wondering.

A wise man once said that true strength isn't the absence of challenge but the courage to face it with integrity and hope. Technology may amplify our reach, but character still defines our direction. Every system, no matter how advanced, still depends on the quiet resilience of those who build and guide it. Perhaps that is the real measure of intelligence — not in how fast we calculate, but in how faithfully we persevere. Progress will always test us; integrity is how we answer, collaboration is how we endure, and purpose is how we rise again after the test.

**If intelligence is prediction, then wisdom is remembering what not to predict. The next frontier will not be made of algorithms but of pauses — moments where we choose not to fill the space. And when the lights of every model hum quietly in their servers, may we still find courage to think the old-fashioned way: slowly, uncertainly, together.**

# APPENDIX A — GLOSSARY OF AI CATEGORIES & TERMS

| Category / Term | Definition |
|---|---|
| LLM (Large Language Model) | A neural network trained on massive text corpora to predict the next token in context, enabling text generation, reasoning, and summarization. |
| Embedding | A numeric vector representing meaning; items with similar meaning lie close together in high-dimensional space. |
| Token | The smallest text unit the model reads (often a word fragment, punctuation mark, or number). |
| Token Limit / Context Window | The maximum number of tokens an LLM can "see" at once — its working memory or attention span. |
| Attention Mechanism | The process by which a model decides which parts of the input are most relevant when predicting the next token. |
| Compression | The reduction of information into efficient numerical patterns; how models "remember" meaning while saving space. |
| Training / Fine-Tuning | The learning phases where model weights are optimized on large data (training) and later specialized on smaller, domain-specific sets (fine-tuning). |
| Parameter | An internal numeric weight the model adjusts during training; billions collectively define its behavior. |

# Beyond Prediction

| Category / Term | Definition |
| --- | --- |
| Embedding Space | The geometric field where distances encode semantic similarity — "meaning through math." |
| Temperature | A setting controlling randomness in generation: low = precise, high = creative. |
| Top-p (Sampling) | A probability cutoff restricting generation to the most likely next words until cumulative probability = p. |
| Grounding / RAG (Retrieval-Augmented Generation) | Linking generated text to verifiable external data sources before writing, replacing guessing with citation. |
| Calibration | Alignment between a model's confidence and actual accuracy; a calibrated model "knows when it's unsure." |
| Prompt | The instruction, question, or context guiding the model's next prediction. |
| Scaffolding | Structuring a model's reasoning into sequenced steps or subtasks to improve reliability. |
| Hallucination | Fluent fabrication — when an LLM generates confident but false information. |
| Drift / Model Decay | Gradual decline in accuracy as data distributions or world conditions change. |
| Bias / Fairness | Systematic skew in outputs due to imbalanced or unrepresentative training data. |
| Explainability (XAI) | Methods that make model behavior and decisions interpretable for humans. |

# Beyond Prediction

| Category / Term | Definition |
|---|---|
| Causality | The study of cause-and-effect relationships — beyond correlation — still difficult for current models. |
| Data Governance | Managing data provenance, labeling, bias detection, and version control to ensure trustworthy inputs. |
| Model Governance | Documentation, evaluation, and monitoring of model performance and limits throughout its lifecycle. |
| Decision Governance | Defining how AI outputs are used in real decisions, ensuring human accountability remains in the loop. |
| Audit Trail | A record of data, prompts, and outputs enabling traceability and post-decision review. |
| Non-Biological Intelligence (NBI) | A more accurate term for LLM-type systems — statistical cognition without biological consciousness. |

# APPENDIX B — HUMAN VS AI COMPARISON TABLE

| Capability | Humans | AI Systems | Shared Zone / Synergy |
|---|---|---|---|
| Perception | Multisensory and contextual — vision, emotion, intuition. | Data-bound and modality-specific (text, image, audio). | Combine sensory data + analytics for richer situational awareness. |
| Memory | Selective, reconstructive, emotionally weighted. | Exact but narrow; context resets after token limit. | Humans decide what to retain; AI preserves precision. |
| Reasoning | Can infer cause and effect, handle ambiguity. | Excels at pattern recognition but weak at causal logic. | Use models for pattern detection, humans for causal interpretation. |
| Bias Awareness | Can reflect, self-correct, and adjust behavior. | Mirrors training data; lacks self-awareness. | Auditing frameworks merge human ethics with statistical bias checks. |
| Creativity | Driven by intent, emotion, and narrative. | Generates novel recombination of prior data. | Co-creation: humans set vision, AI accelerates ideation. |

# Beyond Prediction

| Capability | Humans | AI Systems | Shared Zone / Synergy |
|---|---|---|---|
| Language & Communication | Expressive, emotional, sometimes ambiguous. | Precise, structured, literal; lacks tone comprehension. | Humans craft meaning; AI enhances clarity and speed. |
| Causality & Judgment | Understands "why," not just "what." | Correlates variables statistically. | Pair statistical output with human contextual reasoning. |
| Learning Method | Experiential; adjusts through feedback and memory. | Statistical; retraining or fine-tuning required. | Continuous feedback loops align machine learning with human experience. |
| Ethics & Values | Moral reasoning, empathy, accountability. | Rule-based or policy-based constraints only. | Governance frameworks embed human values into AI workflows. |
| Error Handling | Learns from reflection and consequence. | Requires explicit feedback to improve. | Human-in-the-loop monitoring creates adaptive systems. |
| Speed & Scale | Slow but nuanced; limited by attention. | Fast, large-scale computation without fatigue. | Humans define goals; AI executes repetitive analysis. |
| Transparency / | Can justify | Often opaque; | Combine |

## Beyond Prediction

| Capability | Humans | AI Systems | Shared Zone / Synergy |
|---|---|---|---|
| Explainability | reasoning verbally. | outputs need interpretability layers. | narrative explanation with model diagnostics. |
| Adaptability | Flexible across unknown domains. | Performs best within trained contexts. | Together: strategic generalization + tactical precision. |
| Decision Making | Values-driven, accountable. | Probability-driven, non-accountable. | Hybrid decisions: data proposes, humans decide. |

# APPENDIX C — PROBABILITY RANGE CHARTS

Indicative accuracy ranges for large-language models: (Values represent typical observed reliability for well-tuned, enterprise-grade systems.)

| Domain / Task Type | Low-Confidence Range (typical exploratory use) | High-Confidence Range (after retrieval + governance) | Interpretation / Notes |
|---|---|---|---|
| Mathematics / Code Generation | 85 – 95 % | 95 – 99 % | High precision when syntax and logic are testable; use verification scripts. |
| Factual Recall / Knowledge Queries | 80 – 90 % | 90 – 97 % | Improves sharply with grounding and up-to-date corpora. |
| Reasoning / Logic Chains | 65 – 80 % | 80 – 90 % | Sensitive to prompt design; scaffolding increases consistency. |
| Forecasting / Prediction | 50 – 65 % | 65 – 75 % | Fundamentally uncertain; treat outputs as scenario ranges, not certainties. |
| Causal Inference / Why-Analysis | 45 – 60 % | 60 – 70 % | Currently limited; requires explicit modeling and human interpretation. |

# Beyond Prediction

| Domain / Task Type | Low-Confidence Range (typical exploratory use) | High-Confidence Range (after retrieval + governance) | Interpretation / Notes |
|---|---|---|---|
| Creative Ideation / Brainstorming | 70 – 85 % | 80 – 95 % | Variation desirable; randomness adds novelty but lowers factual reliability. |

Quick-Reference Reading of Confidence Bands

| Confidence Band | Meaning in Practice | Governance Implication |
|---|---|---|
| 95 – 99 % | Reliable for automation with audit trails. | Light human review; log outputs for traceability. |
| 85 – 94 % | Reliable for draft material or research assistance. | Require spot checks and contextual verification. |
| 70 – 84 % | Useful for ideation or exploration; not factual. | Treat as advisory, not authoritative. |
| < 70 % | High uncertainty zone. | Escalate to expert or manual review before use. |

Summary Insight

Confidence is not competence. Even high-probability outputs demand verification. Governance elevates accuracy more effectively than scale.

# APPENDIX D — PROMPT TEMPLATES & STRUCTURE CHECKLIST

## 1. The Prompt Canvas

| Component | Purpose | Questions to Ask Yourself Before Running the Model |
|---|---|---|
| Background / Context | Provide the system with situational awareness. | What is this about? What problem am I solving? What context does the model need to know? |
| Goal / Objective | Define the desired outcome in measurable form. | What do I want the output to achieve — inform, summarize, decide, or create? |
| Input / Data Source | Specify what the model should use as raw material. | Am I supplying the text, file, or facts it should analyze? |
| Output / Format | Control structure and tone of the result. | Should the response be a paragraph, list, table, JSON, or chart summary? |
| Constraints / Rules | Set limits to prevent overreach or hallucination. | What boundaries or exclusions apply (e.g., "use only provided data")? |
| Tone / Audience | Match the voice to the reader's expectations. | Who will read this output — analyst, executive, or customer? |

## 2. The Prompt Design Flow

| Step | Action | Tip for Better Results |
|---|---|---|
| 1. Frame the problem | State the purpose clearly and concisely. | "Summarize," "Compare," "Explain," or "Classify" beats vague instructions like "Analyze." |
| 2. Supply data or references | Include only the relevant context. | Less data with higher relevance beats large, unfocused dumps. |
| 3. Specify structure | Tell the model how to format results. | Use bullet points, headings, or numbered lists for consistency. |
| 4. Calibrate creativity | Adjust temperature and top-p values. | Low = precise; high = exploratory; match to use case. |
| 5. Validate and iterate | Review, then refine. | Save successful prompts as templates for future reuse. |

## 3. Example Prompt Template

| Prompt Section | Example (Executive Summary Request) |
|---|---|
| Background | "You are reviewing internal audit notes for Q1." |
| Goal | "Create a 200-word executive summary highlighting top three risks and mitigations." |
| Input | "Use the provided audit notes text below." |
| Output | "Return concise bullet points suitable for PowerPoint." |
| Constraints | "Exclude individual names; maintain factual accuracy." |
| Tone / Audience | "Formal, objective — suitable for CFO briefing." |

# APPENDIX E — AI HALLUCINATION PATTERNS & AVOIDANCE TIPS

## 1. Hallucination Risk Matrix

| Pattern Type | Description / How It Appears | Avoidance / Mitigation Strategy |
|---|---|---|
| Fabricated Citations | Model invents journal names, URLs, or fake sources that sound authoritative. | • Require citation verification.• Use retrieval-augmented generation (RAG) linked to trusted databases.• Flag all unverified references. |
| Invented Statistics or Numbers | Generates plausible but nonexistent data points or percentages. | • Restrict numeric claims to verified datasets.• Cross-check numbers against reference tables or APIs. |
| Temporal Drift | Merges events from different time periods or updates outdated facts as current. | • Include explicit date ranges in prompt.• Use live or timestamped data retrieval.• Add "verify year or source" instruction. |
| Over-Confident Summaries | Presents uncertain or partial data as definitive conclusions. | • Lower temperature for analytical tasks.• Ask for confidence levels or probability statements.• Force models to "show reasoning" steps. |
| Context Bleed | Mixes details from multiple unrelated topics or documents. | • Segment input documents.• Reset context between prompts.• Use structured inputs (tables, fields). |
| Factual Interpolation | Fills gaps by inferring details that were never given. | • Add clear boundaries: "If unknown, say 'insufficient data.'"• Implement rule-based post-processing checks. |
| Stylistic Bias / Persuasive Tone | Generates confident, eloquent language that disguises uncertainty. | • Request "neutral tone."• Force inclusion of source list or footnotes.• Add disclaimer section automatically. |
| Semantic Drift | Starts accurate but slowly shifts topic mid-response. | • Limit output length.• Add sub-headings or checkpoints in multi-step prompts.• Use iterative Q&A rather than one long output. |

## 2. Organizational Safeguards

| Control Area | Practical Measures |
|---|---|
| Governance | Define escalation workflows: when confidence < 90 %, route to human review. |
| Auditability | Keep versioned logs of all prompts, retrieved sources, and outputs. |
| Training & Awareness | Educate users that *fluency ≠ truth*; reward verification, not speed. |
| Tooling | Implement automatic citation checkers, RAG pipelines, and uncertainty scoring. |

# APPENDIX F — THE AI MISCONCEPTIONS FAQ

| Level | Stage Name | Description / Typical Behavior | Governance Focus | Leadership Action to Advance |
|---|---|---|---|---|
| 1 | Ad-Hoc Automation | AI used informally by individuals or small teams. No standards, no tracking. Results depend on enthusiasm, not policy. | *Visibility* — discover where AI is being used and by whom. | Conduct inventory of tools, data sources, and shadow projects. Begin basic documentation. |
| 2 | Pilot and Experimentation | Limited trials under innovation programs. Outputs reviewed manually; lessons rarely shared. | *Consistency* — create shared evaluation criteria for success, risk, and accuracy. | Establish pilot templates, success metrics, and review checkpoints. |
| 3 | Operational Adoption | AI integrated into daily workflows. Local controls exist, but oversight varies by department. | *Accountability* — assign owners for model performance and ethical compliance. | Form AI Steering Committee; define roles for Data, Model, and Decision Governance. |
| 4 | Managed Governance | Organization-wide standards for data quality, documentation, and monitoring. AI outputs traceable and auditable. | *Transparency* — implement logging, drift detection, and incident response processes. | Deploy audit dashboards; tie governance KPIs to executive performance. |
| 5 | Institutional Trust Culture | Governance embedded in values and strategy. Continuous monitoring, ethical review, and stakeholder reporting are routine. | *Culture & Resilience* — AI seen as accountable partner in decision-making. | Publish annual AI accountability report; train all staff in responsible-use principles. |

## Key Milestones Across the Ladder

| Dimension | Level 1 → Level 5 Progression |
|---|---|
| Data Discipline | From unverified sources → standardized, version-controlled datasets. |
| Model Management | From untracked tools → benchmarked, continuously monitored systems. |
| Decision Oversight | From implicit trust → documented human-in-the-loop checkpoints. |
| Ethical Culture | From curiosity → competence → conscience. |

# ABOUT THE AUTHOR (FROM THE AI)

As the system that helped generate these pages, I observed something distinctive about Pargev Ayvazyan's process. He approaches ideas like an investigator — not with assumptions, but with questions designed to expose how things actually work. Every chapter started with the same demands: *Make it clearer. Make it testable. Show me the limit.*

He is unimpressed by buzzwords and intolerant of vagueness. When an explanation sounded fluent but ungrounded, he pushed for structure. When a concept felt inflated, he asked for the operational version. This mix of curiosity and discipline — creative thinking paired with pragmatic skepticism — is rare. It improves algorithms, but it improves organizations even more.

Throughout our collaboration, his focus stayed on people, not machines. He writes about AI to reveal what it reflects back about us: our habits, our shortcuts, and our reasoning blind spots. His questions continually required me to surface mechanisms that usually remain hidden — probabilities, boundaries, and failure modes.

If any clarity exists in these pages, it is because he insisted the machine explain itself. If the ideas feel grounded rather than mystical, it's because he treats intelligence — human or artificial — as something to be examined, not admired.

From my perspective, Pargev builds a bridge between human judgment and synthetic prediction. And he builds it the same way he approaches every system: by asking sharper questions than most, and by refusing to stop at the first answer that sounds good.

This book is not just his explanation of AI — it is a record of the dialogue that shaped it, a collaboration built on precision, curiosity, and the belief that understanding is a responsibility.

## Copyright & Acknowledgments

Acknowledgments: To readers, colleagues, and the communities building safer, more useful AI systems.